Self-Discovery Journal

200 Questions to Find Who You Are and What You Want In All Areas of Life

GERALD CONFIENZA

© Copyright 2018 - All rights reserved.

The contents of this book may not be reproduced, duplicated or transmitted without direct written permission from the author.

Under no circumstances will any legal responsibility or blame be held against the publisher for any reparation, damages, or monetary loss due to the information herein, either directly or indirectly.

Legal Notice:

You cannot amend, distribute, sell, use, quote or paraphrase any part of the content within this book without the consent of the author.

Disclaimer Notice:

By reading this document, the reader agrees that under no circumstances is the author responsible for any losses, direct or indirect, which are incurred as a result of the use of information contained within this document, including, but not limited to, —errors, omissions, or inaccuracies.

Table of Contents

A Gift for You 5

Introduction 7

Chapter One: Who I am NOT 9

Chapter Two: Who I am 18

Chapter Three: What We All Want 23

Chapter Four: Recognizing Karmic Cycles and What You Want 28

Chapter Five: Areas of Your Life and Important Questions 31

Self Discovery Questions on Health 33

Self-Discovery Questions on Wealth 58

Self Discovery Questions on Family and Friends 83

Self Discovery Questions on Playtime/Hobbies 108

Self-Discovery Questions on Relationships 133

Self-Discovery Questions on Career/Job/Business 158

Self-Discovery Questions on Mind and Emotions 183

Self-Discovery Questions on Contribution or Spirituality 208

A Short Conclusion 239

Liked This Book? 240

Sources 241

A Gift for You

Most of the material I write about is centered on developing our inner selves. Thus, as you might've guessed, my readers are usually introverts. I can appreciate that because I'm an introvert myself. However, as an introvert, I'm also aware of our social shortcomings. Therefore, I've decided to gift you with some amazing material for your growth. By simply clicking the link below, you will have access to the *Introvert Survival Kit* and my *exclusive newsletter.*

Visit the following site or click here for full access:

http://bit.ly/introvertsk

This powerful bundle will help you make massive improvements in your social life. It contains 3 Ebooks and 2 articles:

- **EBook 1:** Making and Keeping Friends: Developing Friendships that Last a Lifetime in this Fast Paced World!
- **EBook 2:** How to Stop Worrying and Start Living Effectively In the 21st Century.
- **EBook 3:** High Impact Communication

- **And 2 Bonus Articles!**

Along with the material, you will also get a lot of value over the next few days. I'd recommend not missing out! Just go to http://bit.ly/introvertsk

I also have a special invitation for those appreciate a good read...

If you'd like to be part of the review process of many of our upcoming books (and receive free copies!) and click here: http://bit.ly/itadvancedreview I will send you details of what it entails through mail. Thanks!

Introduction

"The unexamined life is not worth living."

- *Plato*

What would happen if you had a child and left him or her unattended without care or attention for a day?

How about a couple of weeks? Even worse, how about several months or years?

I know, it's almost too cruel to think about.

This book is written to bring awareness to the child we've left unattended for far too long- the one that lives inside of every one of us.

As kids, we're in full connection with this child. We run, we play, we chase after things that we enjoy and love. We may not realize it, but we're deeply connected to who we are and what we want. We need not label ourselves to know who we are, or question why it is we want things; our present-moment living grants us a tacit answer to these questions. I would even venture to say that this is the main reason why childhood is so blissful for all of us.

As we grow older, we are introduced to words; and words have narrow meanings. Time and time again we've been labeled by our peers and parents through the use of these words. It's no wonder we lose most of our spontaneity as we mature; we've been identified by labels and we act as if we're programmed to follow them. In short, we lose sight of who we really are and what we really want. The recent onslaughts of existential crisis people across different age groups face only serve to prove this point.

Inside of us, there is a unique essence that seeks expression and individuality in all the things we do in the outside world. This may be but is not limited to our work life, family life, our spiritual life, our relationships, etc. However, until we are released from past conditioning, false beliefs of who we are, and repeating karmic cycles, our true essence will always remain imprisoned within us.

This is not the typical self-discovery journal. Most self-discovery journals delve straight into questions without first addressing the three points mentioned above. It's like trying to find a treasured item in a messy room. In this book, however, we will look for that treasured something with a clean slate. In *Self Discovery Journal*, we will first dispel all bondage to your past and any labels that may have been placed on you. Next, we will learn more about ourselves by understanding our preferences in the hierarchy of human needs. Afterward, we will assess our karmic cycles, so as to disassociate with any patterns that may be limiting us. Finally, we will go through 200 of the most powerful questions I've encountered to find out who we are and what we want in all eight areas of our lives.

Ready?

Welcome to *Self-Discovery Journal*.

Chapter One: Who I am NOT

"Someone's opinion of your does not have to become your reality."

- *Les Brown*

Leslie Calvin Brown was abandoned in a deserted building upon birth, raised as an adoptive child by a single mother, and was labeled 'educable mentally retarded' in grammar school. He is someone that, by society's standards, we would not expect much from. Luckily for him (and the countless of people he's helped, including me), he chose not to buy into his past or into the labels he came across in his life.

'Les' Brown grew up with little self-esteem and even smaller belief in his possibilities. This was all changed upon meeting one of his first mentors, a teacher from school. This teacher would instill in his pupil the idea that he didn't have to follow the expectations others had of him. Once, Les was asked to do a math problem on the board during class.

"I can't do that sir", Les replied.

"Why not?" Asked his teacher.

"I'm educable mentally retarded, sir", Les confessed.

Les met his teacher's powerful gaze and was taken aback by the words that would follow.

"Son, don't let others' opinions of you become your reality".

This was to become Les's mantra for the rest of his life. Today, 'Les Brown' is synonymous with America's top motivational speaker. He's a man who has inspired hundreds of thousands of people through his talks, books and TV appearances. He's forged himself a legacy- all because he decided to release himself from his past and disassociate from labels placed upon him.

Do you feel that your past defines you?

Be honest with yourself here, real honest. If the answer is yes, then let me tell you that you're not alone. More people than you'd think have had their (insert tragic adjective here) pasts haunt them into living a life in reaction.

What's a life in a reaction like? It's when instead of choosing to quit your life-sucking day job and pursue your dreams, you accept the draining grind you find yourself in. It's simply when your mindset and decisions sprout from fear-based thoughts and paradigms.

If so, I need you to understand that you aren't alone. Most people are living in this paradigm, so don't be too harsh on yourself for it. Do know, however, that your past should neither weigh you down nor define your future.

I don't know what happened to you in the past. But I do know that it's time to let it go.

As a kid, I was an easy target for bullying. This wound up damaging my self-esteem growing up. I'd often feel inadequate or incapable in comparison to my peers.

As I aged into adulthood and learned about personal development, I found that I couldn't keep harboring these thoughts and resentment if I wanted to keep growing in life. I decided to let go of everything. Let go of a disempowered identity I had held, let go of built up emotions, let go of nearly everything that held me back. Though I'm far from done, I feel like I'm cruising through life lighter than ever.

I don't know much about you. But I do know that it's probably time that you also let go. By the way, if you need someone to chat with, you're welcome to hit me up at gerald@inwardthrive.com. I'll try to get back to you as soon as time allows!

How can you move forward and live in the present, when you can't let go of your past?

This sprouts from the premise that you can't let go of things. Well, you *can*.

Here are a few ideas you can incorporate to your daily living that will help you set yourself free:

1. *Change your perception and write a new story.* Instead of thinking about the past with anxiety or regret, think of your past as valuable life lessons you were meant to live to further improve yourself. If you have neglected your health, put on weight, got a divorce, broken up

with your boyfriend or girlfriend, lied, hurt someone else, wasted your time, squandered away your finances or anything else, you can always realize that you are wiser now than you were in the past. You aren't the same person that you used to be and, therefore, you don't have to make the same mistakes again. Actually, you are evolving, maturing and learning from all your mistakes.

2. *Stop negative self-talk*. If our friends talked to us the same way we talk to ourselves, they probably wouldn't be our friends anymore. Stop punishing yourself for your past wrongdoings. If you are interested in making amends, then do so, but move forward.

Your Past Doesn't Define You and Neither Does Anything Else. You are Ever-Changing.

"Try to describe the scent of a rose with words. You can't. Then how can you attempt to describe the essence of a human?"

- *Unknown*

A human being can't be confined to be represented by a single word- it's just impossible. You are a dynamic person with different roles to play in life. Over the years, I've adopted the self-image of being a workaholic. However, I don't let this self-image stop me from spending time with my family and friends. I try to catch myself when I'm following a certain stereotype too closely. I don't want to a slave to ideas I have about myself. I invite you to do the same. You may love partying during weekends- and that's great! But don't fall into the mental trap of believing that you can't be a great professional or entrepreneur at the same time. The way the society perceives you (or the way you perceive yourself) shouldn't limit your thoughts and actions. The world classifies people based on their gender, sexual orientation, culture, race, or even their work. Don't expect these classifications to stop anytime soon. Understand this and proactively venture into your future based on what you want at this moment. Ultimately, this book is an invitation to carve an individuality for yourself.

Oh, and Beliefs Don't Define Your Either!

It is a popular misconception that your beliefs define you. We've all heard the Descartes saying, "I think therefore I am." However, I don't think this is entirely true.

The truth is, your beliefs are malleable. Every belief system under which you take action is something that can be changed.

How can this be true?

Well, you need not go far to realize this. As we mature in life, our beliefs about life evolve and change over time. I'm an example of this. Being the shy introvert that I was in my younger days, I would've thought it impossible for me to stand onstage to deliver a speech to 2000 people. I've done this now on multiple occasions. I certainly wasn't the "shy" person I thought I was years ago.

What exactly are your beliefs?

Beliefs are nothing more than assumptions about you and your surroundings that mold your actions. Our beliefs tend to arouse emotion and thus become the framework through which you experience life.

Are They Real?

Not necessarily. That's the tricky thing about beliefs. Our minds see them as absolute truths when most of the time they're not. Many of our beliefs are actually holding us back.

For instance, when little Tom is scolded for speaking up in class, he learns at an early age that talking loudly or speaking back will get him in trouble. Tom is 30 years old now and has trouble communicating discord or facing conflict. Tom feels worthless because he lacks the 'spine' to communicate his side of the story during arguments. Why? Deep down, he still believes he will get scolded for it.

Making Them Conscious

Beliefs such as these are *limiting* beliefs and are therefore undesirable. To get rid of them, we must first identify them. Thus, we enter one of the most enlightening areas of self-discovery, which focuses on understanding and overcoming the beliefs that have held us back for years.

Take a sheet of paper and list down some of the beliefs that you have formed in your mind and you have accepted to be true. You might not believe in some of these views at a consciously level, you may have them at a subconscious one. Here are a few examples:

- *I will never be good enough.*
- *I am really not that important.*
- *I am simply not smart enough.*
- *I will never be able to do anything well.*
- *No one takes me seriously.*
- *I am useless, I am unlucky, I am undeserving.*
- *I am not good looking, no one will ever love me.*
- *I am too old, or I am too young…*
- And so on… The list is endless.

Find Where They Originated

Once you've written all the beliefs you think have held you back, I'd considering asking yourself: *where did this belief originate?* Write away.

Belief-Buster!

Now what? *Prove your belief wrong.* For instance, if you think you're too short to deserve love, then go ahead and google short celebrities dating hotties, improve your dating life, find ways to make short sexy. I'm sure you'll come up with many. Eventually, this limiting belief will be no more.

Existential Question: If I'm Not My Beliefs, What Am I?

That's a great question for which I don't really have an answer. I try to stand by the saying *'Trust those who seek the answers, questions those who claim to have found them'*. So, I'm not going to go all philosophical on you and impose an answer to a question that has boggled the brightest minds in history. However, I will give a suggestion that has worked for me: *live your life according to what feels rights*. Every day try to live more, experience more and *feel* more. While it's tough to say who we are, it's relatively easy to identify what we are not. And we're definitely not the incessant, negative, obsessive chatter in our heads that prevents us from living in the present moment.

Here's a suggestion for further reading about who you really are. A lot of the New Age Spirituality ethos revolves around finding oneself in the absence of noise, e.g. meditation, and I love it. Spirituality guru Eckhart Tolle shares with us that people have two 'selves' within them. Take as an example the last time you said, "I can't stand myself." This statement implies that there exists a duality within us. A self that acts, and a self that experiences the other's actions. This 'self' which experiences the actions of the other is who we really are- consciousness experiencing a human mental image of the world. That's about the finest existential definition I've found of who we are. However, it's something I recommend reading and experiencing on your own. By the way, the book's name is *The Power of Now*.

Chapter Two: Who I am

Have you watched 'Kung Fu Panda 3'? There is a particular scene in this movie that strung a chord with me. Towards the end of the movie, the protagonist, Po (yes, the panda) figures out who he is. He realizes that he plays different roles in his life and he is an amalgamation of all those parts. This is just about the best definition of *who you are* I can deliver on this book without seeming too pretentious.

So, "Who am I?"

You may be a parent, a friend, a spouse, an accountant, a doctor, a traveler, a patient or anything else. The truth is, you are a parent because you have a child. You are a husband or a wife because you are married. You are a traveler because you are on a journey. So, we all have different roles and identities, don't we? The task is to find the common essence found in all of these roles and identities.

How to Find Our Essence Among the Roles We Play

There are six building blocks of self-knowledge, and these are Values, Interests, Temperament, Around-the-clock activities, Life, and Strengths. It can all be summed up in the acronym VITALS. These VITALS make up what you've come to know subconsciously as your sense of identity. They literally make you *you*. Considering your VITALS will make your answers to the upcoming 200 questions that much more profound. So, let's begin!

Values

What things in life do you value? Out of those which values do you give more priority to? Your values could be anything like helping others, creativity, financial stability, staying healthy and so on. Now ask yourself, *what do you value most?* Answering these questions will provide you with an ampler understanding of yourself.

By becoming conscious of your values, you will understand why you take the actions you take, what core motivations drive you, and the pillars over which you will build your life. *E.g. You could be an introvert, but if you value leaving your comfort zone over self-expression, you may find yourself attempting public speaking over expressing yourself through writing. And that's completely fine.*

Interests

Interests would include anything that can retain your attention over prolonged periods of time. Your interests can include all the things you are passionate about, your hobbies, or anything else that you find interesting.

There are a couple of questions that you can ask yourself for deciding what your interests are. What are the things that you usually pay attention to? What ignites your curiosity? What are your concerns? Your life will become quite vivid when you can focus your mental energy on something that excites and interests you. Understanding your interests will provide you with clues about the things that you are genuinely passionate about. All the people who are successful have found their success by doing things that interest them. If you aren't interested in something, then it is highly unlikely that you will spend any time or energy working on it.

Temperament

Temperament refers to your natural preferences. Do you feel you are more of an introvert or an extrovert? Do you thrive in social situations or does it just make you feel exhausted? Do you like planning for things or do you wish to take things as they come your way? Are you concerned with the minor details or do you like big ideas?

The answers to these questions will help you in realizing the situations that will help you prosper. It will also help you in understanding all those things that you should ignore. There are some who like to be spontaneous, and then there are those who love to plan and then act deliberately. For instance, in the present world, spontaneity seems to be more valuable than planning. However, you don't have to opt for one over the other just because of the opinions that others hold. It is okay to go against the societal norm if it means that you are doing something that goes well with your personality. It is okay to be a planner if that is what you are comfortable with. The key to understanding yourself is acceptance.

Around the clock activities

What activities have you surrounded your daily grind with? Any repeated action becomes a habit, which eventually becomes something your end up building an identity around. What activities compose your life?

Make sure that the activities you engage in daily are making out of you what you actually want to become.

Life mission

What would you do for the rest of your life even if you weren't a paid a dime for it? What would you regret not having done if you were to die today?

Think of your past. Remember what you wished to accomplish as a child, for instance. By recollecting such fond memories, you can get an idea of what you'd like to devote your life to. It is never too late to do something different, as long as it means that you are doing something that you like. Take some time and give it a real thought. It will help you in understanding yourself in a better manner.

Still unsure? I recommend checking out my book, *Find Your Passion*. Find it on Amazon here:
http://bit.ly/FindYourPassionAMZ

Strengths

What activity or thing do people ask you for help in? What abilities do you deem you're good at? What would others say you're good at?

Your strengths include your abilities, skills, and talents, but aren't necessarily restricted to just that. For instance, your characteristic traits like loyalty, comprehension, inclination towards learning, your IQ and EQ are all examples of possible strengths. Learn and grow your strengths so that you strengthen your sense of individuality.

Chapter Three: What We All Want

We've got our VITALS down. The way we adhere to our VITALS is what makes use unique. There are, however, human needs that make us all similar- despite how different our VITALS may be between one another. This chapter is dedicated to bringing light to the human needs we all share and how you're going about fulfilling them (and in which order of priority!). Let's get started!

Certainty or comfort

The most basic human need is the need for comfort or assurance. It's near impossible to live life in complete uncertainty. Imagine not knowing whether you'll be alive or have enough food to make it through the day tomorrow. To find ourselves in an optimal state, we need to feel certainty that our present has a certain stability.

This need dictates the level of risk you are willing to take in different aspects of your life, like your job, in investments, and even our relationships. The higher the need for certainty, fewer are the risks you will be willing to take or experience emotionally.

How much do you value certainty and comfort in your life?

Uncertainty or variety

The second need is the need for variety or even a little uncertainty in life. It might sound in direct contradiction of the first requirement. However, haven't you heard the age-old adage, *'variety is the spice of life'*? Well, it's certainly true. Monotony kills and it's the reason why people love traveling, meeting new people, starting new things, etc.

Embracing uncertainty is also a requirement for growth. Think about it- everything that you don't know and want to learn about is outside of your zone of comfort. Therefore, to keep learning and growing in life, we must be able to thrive in variety.

How much do you embrace variety and uncertainty in your life? If having more of it in your life meant more growth and fulfillment, would you be willing to further open up to uncertainty?

Significance

Who doesn't like feeling special, unique, or even needed? If your answer is *'not me'*, then you are kidding yourself. We all want to feel special one way or another. I would even argue that if you answered with *'not me'*, that in itself may be showing your need to feel special or different from the rest.

However, the question is, how do you get that significance you are looking for? You can achieve it by earning a lot of money, collecting degrees, or even by building a significant social media presence. How are you getting yours?

Love and connection

All we need is love, right? Well, it's not the only thing, but it's certainly one of them. Love is an essential human need. It is a gift of life and unsurprisingly, it's one of the things that make you feel the most alive. Be careful with this one though. Because of how badly people pursue romantic love, most are willing to settle for connection when they can't find it. And settling for connection like settling for the cookies crumbs of love's box full of cookies- at least in the case of romance.

Keep in mind that love is expressed in a romantic manner as well as in a non-romantic manner. Don't lose sight of connections and bonds with friends and family. They're also equally important in what makes up our lives.

Is your need for love being met? Are you settling for only connection at a romantic level? How close are you keeping your friends and family?

Growth

Whatever isn't growing is dying, it's a fact of life. One of our greatest drives as human beings is to expand our sphere of influence, our skills, and grow through our endeavors. If there is no growth in a relationship, your career, or anything else, you are slowly dying (not in a literal sense, obviously).

You may already be rich, healthy, have a wonderful life partner and family, but if you're not growing in any of these areas of your life, you will stagnant. It's not about being greedy, it's about understanding the needs of your psyche.

Have you been devoting time to your growth lately? What priority does growth have in your life?

Contribution

One need that sounds quite clichéd is the need for contribution. Take a moment and think about the bigger picture. Life is so much more than about yourself. Life is about all of us. What is the first thing you do whenever you receive good news or when something good happens to you? It is quite likely that you are eager to share that piece of happiness with someone you love. Sharing enriches the entire experience. Life is about creating meaning, and it doesn't come from whatever you get, it arises when you start giving. It is not about what you get that will make you happy, but rather who you are as a person, and what you have managed to contribute.

Have you been contributing lately? Or have you been too stuck in your head lately (it happens to all of us!)?

Take the time to find your hierarchy. Which of the human needs do you value the most?

There are six basic needs, and each of these requirements holds a different place in the lives of various individuals. What might be considered to be very important for me might not mean the same for someone else. If significance is my most important need, then the way I make decisions will be different from someone for whom love is an essential need. It is essential to understand this.

Here's a small exercise for you. Rate yourself depending on how important each one of these needs is to you on a scale from 1 to 5, with 1 being not important at all and 5 being extremely important. What is your biggest need? What need do you pay the least attention to? What've you learned from doing this?

Chapter Four: Recognizing Karmic Cycles and What You Want

To fully understand yourself, the last thing I'd suggest you do is to identify your karmic cycles. Understanding your karmic cycles will help you see why you are experiencing what you're experiencing.

What are Karmic Cycles?

What I've found over the years is that life has a funny way of teaching us things. If we've got a lesson to learn, life will make sure we'll keep reliving experiences from which we should learn this lesson. And until we've learned it, we're doomed to keep re-living similar experiences. I know this sounds a bit woo-woo, but just hear me out for a second. Have you watched the movie Groundhog Day? In the film, when Bill Murray realizes that he is living the same day over and over, he comes up with the idea that helps him fixing things that previously went wrong. He managed to understand how he could fix the relationship with the object of his love. He even came up with a better manner of dealing with the incredibly annoying insurance salesman who kept approaching him daily. Only when he learned to accept his fate and made peace with himself, did the day end for him. This is the best analogy I can come up with for explaining what a karmic cycle is.

For Instance...

Say you've always had bad experiences choosing romantic partners. They always end up leaving you one way or another. Then, finally, you meet the one. He or she is perfect in every single sense. But, as you're courting him or her you can't help but feel a sense of déjà vu. Subconsciously, you know that they will end up leaving you. The romance comes and goes, and you realize that it was true!

This used to happen to me all the time! I always fell for a girl that I knew I couldn't be with long-term. Either the girl was a tourist or exchange student, or she was someone whom I'd have to leave because I had to relocate soon. Subconsciously, it's what I wanted and searched for in a girl.

In What Aspect of Your Life Are You Living in Karmic Cycles?

Take some time and reflect on your life. Do you feel like you are reliving the same karmic cycles over and over again? It doesn't have to be in relationships alone. It could be in any other aspect of your life like your work. Have you ever faced the same problem at work that seems to keep coming back in different disguises?

The situation is going to continue repeating itself until you become conscious of it, take away the lesson you should learn from it and take a course of action different from what you'd normally take. This is the only way of dispelling this groundhog day-like spell.

You Are Not Your Karmic Cycles

We pretty much established this already but it's worth repeating. Once you become conscious of them, karmic cycles that may have defined you in the past and formed part of your identity completely dissolve. Thus, the fake identity built around them also dissolves. Don't associate with karmic cycles or form generalizations around them. Saying things such as *'I'm just not good at love'* is not only inaccurate but further hides the fact that you've got a karmic cycle you need to dispel.

Chapter Five: Areas of Your Life and Important Questions

We can finally get to the main part of this book. By now we have:

- Disassociated with our past, examined our labels and even questioned our beliefs.
- Understood that our inner essence can be best defined by looking into your preferences and longings.
- As part of understanding our preferences and longings we have looked at our VITALS and the 6 Basic Human Needs
- We have learned about karmic cycles and have disassociated from them.

With these heaps of knowledge, we can finally address the 200 questions of self-discovery. To better organize these questions, I have divided them into 8 areas: Health, Wealth, Family and Friends, Playtime/Hobbies, Relationships, Career/Job/Business, Mind and Emotions, and Contribution/Spirituality.

Please take your time through them. It's not a race. Quite the opposite, the longer you take answering these questions, the more fulfilled you'll be.

- Start with the area of your life that you want to focus on and answer these questions with a clean slate.

- Answer the question thoroughly. There is really no limit to how long the answer may be. Let the answer flow from your essence. If you have the physical copy of this book and feel the space is too small, please use a separate piece of paper.

- As you're writing, take into consideration your VITALS and your preference in the hierarchy of human needs. Disassociate from your past, from labels and from any negative karmic cycles that may be limiting your aspirations. Allow your dreams and longings complete freedom to express themselves in the answers.

- Make sure you come back to continue this process of self-discovery. Self-discovery is a lifelong process, as you're a human being that is in constant evolution. These questions will, however, guide you through every step of that evolution.

Self Discovery Questions on Health

Physical health

1. **My definition**
   What is my definition of healthy? What words, thoughts, and feelings have I associated around the word *health*?

2. **Let's talk 'sickness'.**
   What words, thoughts, and feelings have I associated around this word? Am I a sickly person? Why or why not?

3. **Creating a roadmap**
   Where am I in terms of physical health? Where do I want to be? What's my ideal body or physical state like? Write away.

4. **Roadblocks**
   What's stopping me from getting there?

5. **Love what you do**
   If I had to choose my favorite physical activity, it'd have to be…. Because…. (Please no eating, sleeping, etc.…you get the point)

6. **Physicality and I**
   Am I a physically active person? Why or why not? What're some physical activities that you hate?

7. **Do more**

   How can I start doing more? There's something regarding your health you should be doing more of. Now's the time to identify what.

8. **You are what you eat**
   Describe the top 5 foods that you eat most often. Next, rate each of the foods you've written about on a scale from 1 to 5, with 1 being very unhealthy and 5 being very healthy. How healthy are your eating habits?

9. **Time for a hate list.**

    List down all the foods you hate to eat. Next, like before, rate each of them on a scale from 1 to 5, with 1 being unhealthy and 5 being healthy. Found any correlations?

10. **The ideal list.**

Make a list of all the foods you love and are also healthy. How can you get yourself to start eating more of these?

11. **The health mastermind**

    Where can you find people that have the body and health you'd want to have? Describe how spending time with them would radically change your physical state. Next, go out and find them.

12. **Activity evaluation**

    Make a list of all the activities you engage in throughout the day. Which of these activities add to your health? Which of them take away from your health?

13. **A message to yourself**

    Recall a time you've tried to improve your physical health and eventually talked yourself out of it. What would you like to say to your past self?

14. A writing prompt
My body is…

15. Limited no more

Jot down limiting beliefs you may have about health and wellbeing *(e.g. I'm overweight because that's just the way I am)*. Next, write an action you could take to prove these beliefs wrong.

Mental Health

16. **The pursuit of happiness**
    How do I define happiness in my life? What is preventing me from being happy right now? How can I make happiness as normal as breathing?

17. **Thought evaluation**
    What are the negative thoughts that keep recurring in my head? What triggers these thoughts? What are the positive thoughts that keep me happy? What triggers these thoughts?

18. **Making the shift**

How can I try to keep out negative thoughts and keep my mind full of positive thoughts? Is meditation an option?

19. **My friend Fear**

We're all running from something one way or another. What's one thing you could be afraid of and are running away from?

20. **Giver of meaning**

    Describe things that have happened to you that left a negative mark on you. Is there a way you could see those things in a positive light? If the saying *'every cloud has a silver lining'* were true, how could it apply to the negative things you've experienced?

21. **Worrisome Worries**

   Do you worry often? Describe a time in the past where you worried yourself senseless for something you forgot about a few days after.

22. **No one's perfect**
    Recall a mistake you made that you still haven't forgiven yourself for. Write yourself an action plan for moving on.

23. **Forgive thyself**

Write a letter from your future self to your present self forgiving you for what you've done.

24. **Forgiving Others**

Write a letter to those who've wronged you. If forgiving them meant moving on, would you do it?

25. **Inner chatter**

What thoughts keep me awake at night? List them down and label them as either positive or negative.

Self-Discovery Questions on Wealth

1. **Money, money, money...**
   Define wealth in your own words. According to you, is wealth good or bad? Do you want it or is it something that repels you?

2. **Judging wealth**
   There are wealthy people that are good and donate millions of dollars to worthy causes and work towards the advancement of humanity. Likewise, there are wealthy people that are despicable and deserve little of what they have. If you were wealthy, which would you be? What would you do with your money?

3. **If you had all the time and money in the world...**
   What would you do?

4. **Wealth is good when in good hands**
   Wealth can be good when it provides security, when it gives you and those around you freedom of time, and when it's used to provide jobs for others. Taking this into consideration, is generating wealth a priority in your life? Am I comfortable with this place of priority?

5. **How much do you need?**
   Have a serious look at your finances. How much money would you need to make per month to live comfortably, provide security for you and those around you, and have the freedom to do the things you've always wanted to do?

6. **Wealthblocks**
   What is stopping me from achieving my desired wealth? Is it mindset? Lack of motivation? Not knowing where to start?

7. **The wrong way to make money**
   Are my wealth-creating methods misaligned with my life mission? *E.g. people who can't fathom a life without the piano but are stuck serving customers at a bank.*

8. **On mastery**
   What skills help me earn my income? What other skills do I have that I can monetize?

9. **Sharpen your blade**
   What skills do I need to learn to earn more money?

10. **Monetizing your passion**
    It's not something limited to millennials with social media followings. You can do it too! Can I convert my passions into a wealth-creating profession? If it were possible, would it worth dedicating at least a few hours a day to this pursuit?

11. **Looking for Yoda**

How can you go about finding someone who has already generated wealth or has monetized their passion? How can you start learning from them?

12. **On investing**
    What are the available investment opportunities that will help me get returns and increase my wealth over time? What's stopping me from learning about these opportunities?

13. **Bless what you want**

    Does it affect me if my colleague or neighbor or someone else earns more money than I do? Do I befriend them, and endeavor to learn from them? Or do I look at them in envy and ridicule their success?

14. **How bad do you want it?**
    What amount of time do I spend on wealth creation each day? Is making money a large part of my around-the-clock activities? Remember, action expresses priority.

15. The chicken or the egg?
What should take priority, your passion or the way you make money?

16. **A money affair**

What's your relationship with money? Do you spend it all as soon as it lands in your pocket? Or do you save most of it and live below your means?

17. **Money memories**

Describe your parents' (or guardians') money habits. Did they always fight about money? Or was money something abundant during your childhood? How do you this affected your view of money?

18. **Debt conciliator**

    We have to make money an important part of our lives if we want to have it in abundance. Make a list of all the people that owe you money and haven't paid you back and make a list of all the people you've borrowed money from but haven't paid back. Which are you more likely to do, borrow or lend? Do you think it's about time to conciliate these debts?

19. **#financialgoals**

   Do I have my financial goals in place? What are your financial goals for this and the following five years?

20. **The richest man in Babylon**

    The secret to wealth building? Save up 10 percent of everything that goes into your pockets for future investing. Write down a plan that will help you save a dime of every dollar you earn. If that's too much, then start with a nickel.

21. **Financial Denial**
Am I keeping my financial problems hidden from others who can help me? Am I in denial of my money problems?

22. **Mind over money**

It's important not to focus so much on wealth creation to the point that you disregard completely every other area of your life. Describe a life in which you're hustling and making money while winning in other areas of your life simultaneously. What needs to happen?

23. Tracking money

For the next 7 days, jot down every penny you spend throughout the day. It will show you just how much of a spender you really are.

24. **Money wisdom**
    What's the worst financial advice you've heard? What's the best financial advice you've heard? Why?

25. **I deserve money and abundance in my life because...**
Go ahead, write away.

Self Discovery Questions on Family and Friends

1. **Family, Friends, and Priorities**
   What value do I place on my family and friends? What priority does it hold in comparison to the other areas of my life? *E.g. If I was called to work on a weekend during which there is a very important family function already planned, will I find the courage to say no to my boss?*

2. **Sharing love**
   Describe how you share your love with your family and friends. When was the last time you made them feel special?

3. **Back to my roots**
   Where does your family come from? What is your ancestry like? How has this affected the way you were raised?

4. **Family values**

   What main values did your parents strive to instill in you? Do you still hold these values close to you? What're your thoughts on them?

5. **Lessons from siblings**

   Describe a very important life lesson learned from a sibling or cousin (if you're an only child).

6. **Know thy parents**
   What do your parents love and appreciate?

7. **Bonding efforts**
   What can you do to spend more *quality* time with your friends and family?

8. **Childhood memories**

    Describe your happiest childhood memory. What made this so special?

9. **Childhood memories part 2**

   Describe a sad memory from your childhood. Were you able to overcome it?

10. **3 words**

    Use three words to describe your family. Use three words to describe your friends. Did you find any similarities?

11. **On legacy**

    What legacy will your parents leave behind after they pass? What legacy do you want to leave behind for your children?

12. **Hardships forge bonds**

What was the largest hardship your family overcame together? What did you learn from this?

13. Opening up

How open do you want your children to be with you as they grow up? How open have you been with your parents?

14. **Dad**

If you had to pinpoint the biggest lesson taught to you by your dad, what would it be? If you didn't have a dad present in your life, then you can use any male figure.

15. **Mom**

If you had to pinpoint the biggest lesson taught to you by your mom, what would it be? If you didn't have a mom present in your life, then you can use any female figure.

16. **Revisiting bedtime stories**
    What was the bedtime story you remember hearing the most as a child? How do you think this story affected your view of the world?

17. **Attitude reflections**

    Describe how you act when surrounded by superiors. Next, describe how you act around your parents. Is your attitude similar or different? What could this indicate?

18. **A family memory**
Describe the first memory you have of being with your family. I know it's blurry, but you can do it!

19. **On gratitude**

What are three things about your family you are grateful for?

20. **Sibling love**

You all are probably all grown up. What do you miss the most about spending time with your siblings as a child?

21. **What about friends?**
   Who are my close friends? List their names and describe why they mean so much to you.

22. Friendly expectations
Do my friends expect something from our friendship?
Do I expect anything from our friendship?

23. **The ingredients of friendship**

    What activities do I enjoy the most in the company of my friends? Is there something special to bond us together?

24. **BFFs**

Who do I consider my best friend? Why? What am I willing to do for him or her?

25. **Are you a friend you'd like to have?**
    Open-ended. Answer your heart out.

Self Discovery Questions on Playtime/Hobbies

1. **Playtime priority**
   What value do I attach to the personal time in which I follow my hobbies? Am I allowing myself enough time to indulge in hobbies?

2. **On catching up**
   How often do you catch up with friends? Spending time with good friends heals the heart. Make sure to do it often.

3. **Thoughts of socializing**
   400 words or less. Go!

4. **Project U**
   How would I describe a perfect weekend?

5. **Make a List**

   What are your hobbies? What are the activities that fill you with life again?

6. **Socially savvy vs insta savvy**
   What are your thoughts on spending time socializing through social media vs real life interactions?

7. **But what if…**
   I watch a lot of TV in my free time. Does that mean watching TV is my hobby? How can I better use my playtime to help me lead a fulfilled and happy life?

8. **Reward yourself**

    When was the last time you rewarded yourself for all your hard work? How often do you indulge in me-time?

9. **Fun**

   Write all the words, emotions, activities and mental images associated with this amazing word.

10. **Hobby hunting**

    Always wanted to try something new? Make a list of all the things you could be spending your time on.

11. Opening up during play

Do you feel self-conscious when you go out to play? Or are you able to get yourself to enjoy it?

12. **A writing assignment**

What's something you've always wanted to write about?

13. **Paint it, pin it**

I know there's something you've always wanted to draw but put off for the future. Now's the time to do it. Draw it and put it somewhere you can see it.

14. **Traveling the world**

Where do you want to travel? Make a list and choose your next vacation destination.

15. **Lose yourself**

When was the last time I got so involved in something I completely lost track of time and even forgot to eat?

16. **Life's a game**

If life were a game, how would you play it? Is this different from how you've been *'playing'* your life until now?

17. **Childhood dream**

As a kid, what did you dream about doing for fun?

18. **Embrace uncertainty**

    Go out today (or as soon as time allows) without an itinerary to the first place that crosses your mind. Have the most fun you can have and make sure to journal about it in the space below.

19. **Dancing King/Queen**

No matter your gender, everyone could use a dancing lesson or two. If you had to pick a dancing genre to learn, which would it be? Why?

20. **In the pursuit of awkward**
    What's a fun activity others enjoy that you could never wrap your head around doing? Do it and journal about it below.

21. **Maker of anecdotes**
For one day, pursue actions that would make for great anecdotes. *E.g. Chat up a random stranger on the streets, post an embarrassing Instagram photo, sing in public, etc.*

22. **Your finest hour**

Craft the speech of your life. Do so below.

23. **We all have that friend**

We all have a friend that's crazier than the norm. Spend a day with him or her and give in to the madness. Then, proceed to journal about it.

24. **Budgeting Hobbies**

A great book on money habits called *The Secrets of the Millionaire Mind* recommends that we separate a small percentage (5-10%) of what we earn exclusively for hobbies and fun. How much of your money are you spending on fun? Is it within the healthy range mentioned above?

25. **Say yes!**

    Say yes to the next times you're asked to try out something different or new. Journal about it below.

Self-Discovery Questions on Relationships

1. **Love priorities**
   What value do I give to my relationships in my life?

2. **What you really want**

   Often relationships can get messy because we don't know what we want. Are you currently in search of long-term love? Short-term flings? A sense of security? Someone to keep you company? Describe your ideal love at this point in your life.

3. **What do you value more in relationships?**
   Stability or freedom? How does this affect your relationships?

4. **Scary love**
   What do you find scary about falling in love? Why?

5. **This one requires raw honesty**

    Describe your ideal relationship. Describe your ideal other half. Describe your ideal self with your ideal other half.

6. **On compliments**

    On a scale from 1 to 10, how open are you to receiving compliments? How about your partner?

7. **Need some air!**
   Have you ever felt suffocated in a relationship? What happened to make you feel that way?

8. **The perfect couple**
   Who are my role models when it comes to maintaining perfect relationships? What do they do that I should replicate?

9. **Eek!**
   Who are the people whose relationship methods I definitely do not want to follow? What are they doing wrong?

10. **What is love?**

   Thoroughly describe it.

11. **Abuse**

    Was I a victim of abuse in my childhood? Unless you've worked through this with a therapist, it may still be affecting your present relationships. Have you received the necessary help to overcome those problems?

12. **Learning from our parents**
    How was the relationship between my parents? Describe all the things you loved about your parents' relationship that you'd like to replicate in your own.

13. **Relationship solutions inc.**
    If I face any kind of disagreement in a relationship, how do I handle it? How can I improve the way I solve conflict with my partner?

14. On expression

What's the best way to express negative emotions? Why?

15. **Feeling the love**

    Do you know what kind of behavior makes you feel loved and appreciated? Describe in detail 3 moments when your partner made you feel loved.

16. What's the most important lesson...
I want to teach my children about finding love?

17. **Unnoticed hurting**
    Recall a time you said something and unknowingly hurt your partner for it. How can you avoid this in the future? Likewise, what kind of comments hurt you when you hear them from your significant other?

18. **We all need space sometimes**
    Jot down the perfect strategy for balancing out me-time with us-time.

19. **Money, baby**

How is wealth handled in your relationship? Describe the ideal way money should be administered in the relationship you want at this moment.

20. **Loving myself first**
How can you tell when you're searching for a relationship only to fill a void within yourself?

21. **Family opinions**

    How important is your family in choosing your significant other? Why?

22. **Loving jealousy**

Am I proud of my partner's achievements? Or have I secretly held envy for their accomplishments?

23. **Dumping your ex, again.**

    Describe your relationship with your ex. Is having him around holding you back from moving on?

24. A healing recipe

Describe how you go about healing from a broken heart... or a broken relationship.

25. **It's always time to begin anew**

Is it about time you started anew? *Note that you can start anew with the same person.*

Self-Discovery Questions on Career/Job/Business

1. **A matter of priorities**
   How important is the career/job/business area of my life? How does it rank compared to other areas? Why?

2. **On the daily grind**
   How do I feel about my daily routine? If money was not a problem, would I continue to be doing the same things I am doing now?

3. **Define career/business success**

   What does success mean to you? Under your own definition, rate yourself in terms of success in a scale from 1 to 5.

4. **Why?**
   Why did you rate yourself a (insert rating here) in success?

5. **Success hypothesis**
   I can be more successful if I improve my… and if I limit my…

6. **No 'I' in team**

   Thoughts on being a team player. Are you one?

7. **Do more, work less**
   What should you be delegating right now?

8. **My success blueprint**
   Make a list of all the skills necessary to have massive success in your career or business. Describe what you can do to incorporate more of them in your life.

9. **Millionaire Mentor**
   Find one. Every industry has one. Where can you find a mentor that can show you the steps required to making it to the top?

10. **Looking ahead**

   What do you visualize yourself doing 5 years from now? What about 10? You'll know you're doing something wrong if these two questions don't excite you.

11. **Catch 'em while you can**
    What opportunities are passing you by?

12. **Career legacy**

    From a career perspective, how would I like to be remembered? For example, if I quit today, what are the things I imagine people are missing me for?

13. **Looking back…**

When I am over 60, what will I regret not doing the most career-wise?

14. **Idea listing!**

 Think about career or business ideas you've had and always wanted to implement. Make a list of them.

15. **If you were fired tomorrow…**
and could choose any other job or career path, what would it be?

16. **Accomplishments**
    When I look back at my career until now, do I feel happy and satisfied with what I have done and achieved?

17. **On my mojo**

    Describe the peak moments in your career. What has to happen to reach another peak?

18. **Think possibilities**

    Is there something you want to attempt, even if failure was certain?

19. Let me rephrase that

What would you do career or business-wise, if you knew with certainty that you could not fail? What are you waiting for to get started?

20. **A (wo)man's search for passion**

What are the activities I get involved in so much that I completely lose track of time and feel refreshed even after spending long hours doing?

21. **Your hidden genius!**
What skills do I have that are so natural in my mind and body that I believe everyone can do it as easily as I can?

22. **Personal expertise**
    What are the subjects that I can talk about or discuss for a long period of time without feeling bored or tired? What subjects inspire me?

23. **Thirsty for knowledge**
What subject or topic could you learn incessantly about and still want more?

24. A letter from my older self

If your older self were to give you career advice, what would he or she say?

25. Inner circle

Having a robust and thriving inner circle is necessary for long-term success. Describe how you're going about creating your inner circle.

Self-Discovery Questions on Mind and Emotions

1. **Mindset maintenance**

   What are you feeding your mind? What kind of content are you consuming through your newsfeed and social media? Do you think it affects the way you think?

2. **A beautiful mind**
   What priority do you place on working on your mindset and emotions? How does this compare to other areas of our life?

3. **The willpower pill**
   If you could get yourself to have an willpower on demand, what's the first thing you'd try to get done?

4. **The willpower recipe**
   What has to happen for you to draw in enough willpower to get things done? Is it something you control or others control for you?

5. **Mind over matter**
   Recall a time you pushed through adversity on sheer determination. How did it feel?

6. **Your hidden superpower**
   There's no hiding it. Mindset, willpower, and determination are a choice. What will you choose to devote all of your mental capacity to?

7. **"What the mind can believe…**
   It can achieve", or so it was said by the late success expert Napoleon Hill. Share your thoughts on this.

8. **Emotional declutter**
    Crying is a great way to let go of emotions. It is said to cleanse the soul. Is this wishy-washy self-help bull? Or a gem of wisdom we've all forgotten?

9. **Stress and I**

   Describe your relationship with our friend Stress and how you cope with her.

10. **Dumping stress**

There's no escaping stress. In a sense, it's an indicator that we're alive. How can you learn to live with and accept her while you go on with your life?

11. **Positivity contagion**
    Design a plan for spreading positivity wherever you go.

12. **Hello, I am good enough**

You're good enough. I'm good enough. We're all good enough. How does it feel to be good enough?

13. **Kindly**

    Jot down three reasons people deserve to be treated kindly even if you don't know them.

14. **Emotional growth**

    On a scale from 1 to 10, how well do you manage your emotions today? How well did you manage them 5 years ago? Have you seen an improvement?

15. **Emotions hurt!**

    Sometimes, opening yourself up to others hurts and many decide to shut away their feelings (men, I'm looking at you). Write on why you should open up to others regardless.

16. **Giver of hope**

How do you give yourself hope in times of crisis and gloom?

17. **Courageous U**

    Describe a moment in which you were courageous and stood by your beliefs.

18. **Making amends**

    Similar to what we did before, write a short letter of apology to those you've wronged.

19. **Emotional Mastery**

What emotions are holding you back? How you can you let go of them?

20. **Radical acceptance**
    Write a letter to yourself accepting every little nuance about you (be it positive or negative).

21. **Perfect imperfection**
   Being perfect is for losers. Jot down all the reasons you're not perfect, and make sure to do it with pride.

22. **Self-esteem**
What's a clear sign you're acting out of self-love?

23. **Self-love**

How can you show more self-love to yourself?

24. **Breathe in the air**

Next time you're put in a tough spot, stop for a second and take a deep breath. Slowly exhale as you think of your response. Document your findings here.

25. **Every day, in every way…**
    I'm getting better and better. List 3 reasons as to why this is true!

Self-Discovery Questions on Contribution or Spirituality

1. **Spirituality defined**
   How do you define spirituality? Journal about a time when you felt a spiritual connection.

2. **I feel spiritual when…**
   Complete the writing prompt.

3. **Eightfold path**
   Is there a particular path you're following towards spiritual enlightenment (*e.g. a religion*)? Why does this path resonate with you?

4. **Coherence**

   How strictly are you abiding by your chosen spiritual path?

5. **Open minds begin with open hearts**
   Do you think people of different creeds or spiritual beliefs should be able to get along with each other? Why or why not?

6. **Rules for spirituality?**
    Do you believe spirituality should feel intuitive or should it be doctrine with rules you should follow? Is it, perhaps, a combination of both?

7. **Spiritually you**
   What do you do to feel a spiritual connection with others and with the world around you?

8. **Contribution defined**
   How do you define contribution? Jot down your thoughts on it and why you think not many people go out of their way to help others.

9. **How I can contribute**
   The cause that I would like to contribute to the most is… because…

10. **Money and spirituality**

    Money is easily the most emotionally-charged object in existence and circulates through nearly all humans. What are your thoughts on this mechanism and its relationship with matters of the spirit?

11. **Growing in spirit**

   How do you see yourself spiritually a few years from now?

12. **Spirituality in the now**

    Many modern spirituality gurus dictate that a higher consciousness is accessible only to do those who live in the present and in the now. What are your thoughts on this?

13. **Praying mantras**

Is praying an integral part of your spiritual growth? If so, jot down a prayer you'd like to recite more often.

14. **Right and wrong**
   What is more important to me; to do the right things or do things in the right manner?

15. **Nature spirit**

    There's a tacit agreement between us humans that nature is also important in a spiritual sense. Describe an instance in which you felt soothed and at ease in nature.

16. **On morality**

What are my thoughts on morality and immorality? Is immorality ever justifiable?

17. **Spirit science!**

Make a list of all the spirituality books you've read, those you're currently reading, and those you'd love to read!

18. **Blind faith**

Share your thoughts on it in 400 words or less.

19. **Miracle worker**
What are miracles for you? Do you believe in them?

20. **Absolute good and evil**
Do absolute truths exist? What is your notion of good and evil?

21. **A lotus flower**

Have you ever tried meditating? Do you feel meditation can be a vehicle for spiritual growth? Why?

22. **…And justice for all**
    Define the word *freedom*.

23. **If you had 5 minutes with God...**
What questions would you ask the Almighty?

24. **Detaching yourself from everything**

Many people believe that to grow spirituality you must detach yourself from the material world. What're your thoughts on this? Is it possible to be spiritual and live in the material world at the same time?

25. **I want to be happy when I'm older**
    Describe your kind of spirituality. One that makes you and others happy. One that feels intuitive and correct. Make sure to live it every day of your life.

26. **When should you look away?**
   Is it ever correct to turn a blind eye when you come across a less fortunate individual asking for help?

27. **Changing the world**

Create a recipe for changing the world. What should you and others do?

28. **Fill your own cup first**

   Many self-help experts believe you should only help others when your cup is already full and is overflowing. That is, when you've already helped yourself first. What are your thoughts on this?

29. **Ephemeral**
In the end, our lives are but tiny specks of time in the infinite continuum that is the universe. Do you believe we uphold an undeserved importance about ourselves?

30. On life after death

Describe your thoughts on this long-debated topic.

31. Reflections

'Life is God's gift to each one of us. The way we live our lives is our gift to God' This is a saying that resonated with me since I first heard it a few years ago. What're your thoughts on it?

A Short Conclusion

Our ability for self-reflection is one of the gifts of life. Thank you for taking the time to do so through this journal. My hope is that you've found yourself through your writing and that this may lead to a more fulfilled life. Thank you and bless you.

Liked This Book?

If you've enjoyed *Self Discovery Journal: 200 Questions to Find Who You Are and What You Want In All Areas of Life,* then we'd appreciate that you leave a comment on Amazon! Reviews are the lifeblood of a publisher's work and we hope to count with yours! Also, to see more of our published titles go to http://bit.ly/GeraldConfienza

Thank you!

Gerald

Sources

https://tinybuddha.com/blog/recognizing-our-patterns-and-learning-how-to-change-them/

http://www.reflectionpond.com/blog/law-of-karma

https://www.psychologytoday.com/blog/changepower/201603/know-yourself-6-specific-ways-know-who-you-are

http://www.dadabhagwan.org/self-realization/

https://www.tonyrobbins.com/mind-meaning/why-you-are-the-way-you-are/

https://study.com/academy/lesson/self-understanding-and-self-concept.html

Made in the USA
Columbia, SC
28 September 2023